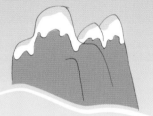

Snow-Covered Peaks

What are Bodhisattvas like?

Retold from the Buddha's Teachings on
The Land of Bliss

Instilling Goodness Books

Buddhist Text Translation Society

Snow-Covered Peaks
What are Bodhisattvas like?

Retold and adapted by Bhikshuni Jin Rou from

Luis O. Gomez, *The Land of Bliss: The Paradise of the Buddha of Measureless Light: Sanskrit and Chinese Versions of the Sukhāvatīvyūha Sutras*. Copyright © 1996 by University of Hawaii Press. Reprinted by permission of University of Hawaii Press.

Chinese translation (for reference) by Bhikshuni Jin Jing
Edited by Angela Morelli
Illustrated by Shramanerika Gwo He
Designed by Levendivin

Published and translated by:
Buddhist Text Translation Society
4951 Bodhi Way, Ukiah, CA 95482
www.buddhisttexts.org

Buddhist Text Translation Society
4951 Bodhi Way, Ukiah, CA 95482
www.buddhisttexts.org
info@buddhisttexts.org

Library of Congress Cataloging-in-Publication Data

Names: Jin Rou, Bhikshuni, author.
Title: Snow-covered peaks : what are Bodhisattvas like?
Description: First English edition. | Ukiah, CA : Buddhist Text Translation
   Society, 2016. | "Retold and adapted by Bhikshuni Jin Rou from Luis O.
   Gomez' The Land of Bliss: The Paradise of the Buddha of Measureless Light."
Identifiers: LCCN 2015027586| ISBN 9781601030771 (pbk. : alk. paper) | ISBN
   9781601030788 (ebook)
Subjects: LCSH: Bodhisattvas--Juvenile literature.
Classification: LCC BQ4695 .J56 2016 | DDC 294.3/4432--dc23
LC record available at http://lccn.loc.gov/2015027586

बोधसित्त्व

Bodhisattva

(Bo-dee-sat-va)

Bodhi means enlightenment. *Sattva* means living being.

Bodhisattvas are enlightened and help others to become
enlightened. They are the Buddha's helpers. Helping
is their job. They are wise, kind and caring. No matter
what the trouble is, they are there to help.

They may appear as a wise elephant to help another
elephant. They may appear as a friend to make one
happy. Whenever we think of them, they fill our hearts
with the light of their great compassion. But they never
brag or let us know who they are.

One day the Buddha was sitting in the shade of a sala tree. His dearest disciple Ananda came and asked him, "O Kind and Wise Buddha, what are Bodhisattvas like?"

The Buddha smiled warmly and said, "Listen carefully and I will tell you."

Bodhisattvas are like snow-covered peaks, because they radiate goodness that is pure and lofty.

They are like the great earth, because they nurture all things equally.

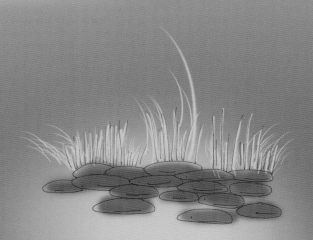

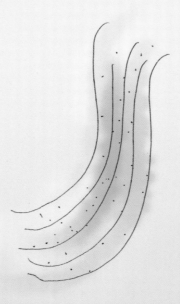

They are like pure water,
because they wash away our troubles.

They are like the great wind,
because they move freely
throughout the world and do not
cling to anything.

They are like a white lotus blossom,
because they are not spoiled by
anything in the world.

They are like
a diamond mountain,
because Mara, the Evil One,
cannot shake them.

They are like a great rain, because they sprinkle every heart with the sweet teachings of the Buddha.

They are like the king of fire, because they burn up the firewood of pride. They are not arrogant at all.

They are like the banyan, the king of trees, because they shelter us with loving-kindness.

They are like the golden-winged garuda,
the king of birds, because they are the most
magnificent of all.

They are like the udumbara flower, because they are rare to come across.

Note: Legend says that the udumbara flower blooms once every 3,000 years.

They are like migratory birds, because they take only what they need and do not hoard anything.

They are like the king of bulls, because no one can conquer them.

They are like the king of elephants, because they are tame and majestic.

They are like the king of lions, because they are brave and noble.

They are like the sky, because their
kindness covers us all.

The Buddha said, "Ananda, if everyone did the things that Bodhisattvas do, they would become Bodhisattvas too. With their eyes and hands, they can help others. With the light of their compassion, they can bring peace and happiness to the world.

Instilling Goodness Books

The Kind Monk

Snow-Covered Peaks

Human Roots, Buddhist Stories

No Words—(long hyphen)Teachings of the Buddha

The Light of Hope (English and Chinese)

The Awakened One (English and Chinese)

The Giant King Turtle (English, Chinese, Spanish)

The Legend of Mahadutta (English and Spanish)

The Spider Thread (English and Chinese)

Under the Bodhi Tree

Come Back, O Tiger!

Instilling Goodness Books is a branch of the Buddhist Te
Translation Society. Its aim is to bring an understanding of Buddhis
to all children in the world, in their own languages. Ancient storie
are retold and illustrated by modern educators, artists, and childre
alike. The books and materials contain lessons and activities i
spiritual, moral, social and cultural development.

Headquarters is located at the City of Ten Thousand Buddhas, a spiritual community founded by Venerable Master Husan Hua from China. It is also the home of Dharma Realm Buddhist University and Instilling Goodness Elementary and Developing Virtue High schools.

Emphasis in our schools is placed on moral virtue and spiritual development in addition to the required academic curriculum. Bilingual education in Chinese and English are also offered. Boys and girls are educated separately to avoid distractions and preserve their pure natures. Summer camps are held every year. For information about our schools and summer camp, please visit our website at *www.igdvs.org*

Dharma Realm Buddhist Association
www.drba.org/www.drbachinese.org

Venerable Master Hua's words to children:

Young friends, you are like young trees growing taller day by day, and in the future you will become the pillars of your country. You should do great things and work for world peace.

First of all you must learn to be a good person. What is a good person? A good person is filial to his parents, respectful to his teachers and helpful to his friends and his country. Under the leadership of good people, a nation will become prosperous, strong and peaceful. It is your responsibility is to stop the wars in the world so the people will be safe and happy, well-fed and well-clothed. Then the world will be one of great harmony.

Adapted from *Talks on Dharma,* Volume 9, page 3